Time-Saving Ideas for

Your Church Sign

1001
ATTENTION-GETTING
SAYINGS

By Verlyn D. Verbrugge

ZONDERVAN™

GRAND RAPIDS, MICHIGAN 49530 USA

Your Church Sign
Copyright © 1999 by Verlyn D. Verbrugge

Requests for information should be addressed to:
Zondervan, *Grand Rapids, Michigan 49530*

Library of Congress Cataloging-in-Publication Data

Verbrugge, Verlyn D.
 Your church sign : 1,001 attention-getting sayings / Verlyn D. Verbrugge.
  p. cm.
 ISBN-10: 0-310-22802-6 (pbk.)
 ISBN-13: 978-0-310-22802-8 (pbk.)
 1. Church signs. 2. Advertising — Churches. I. Title.
BV653.7.V47 1999
254'.4 — dc21   99-314413
                                                        CIP

Interior design by Nancy Wilson

Printed in the United States of America

05 06 07 08 09 10 11 • 15 14 13 12 11 10 9 8

To John, Dot, Ted, Maria, and Sarah

Who have done a marvelous job keeping me human

Contents

Preface

The suggestion for this book came from some of my colleagues at Zondervan who have been personally challenged by many of the church sign captions they have seen. They felt strongly that there was a need for a collection of good sign captions. Since I have been changing the church sign at the Woodland Drive-In Church for the past five years and already had a list of more than a hundred captions, I volunteered to work on the book. As I began doing so, I discovered that the first hundred are the easiest to get!

This collection of more than a thousand captions would not have been possible without a lot of help from people passing on sign captions to me. When I first took on the task of changing captions on our church sign, my wife, Lori, who has always had a way with words, assisted me by writing down captions she had seen and by developing some of her own. Several people of the Woodland Drive-In Church have also been feeding me captions, especially Tom Hielkema, Shirley Van Noord, and Sue Molter. Mike Hoffman and Jonathan Petersen, fellow employees at Zondervan, have surfed the Internet and come up with a number of sayings. Helen Grasman, who works with my wife at a local quilt store, has also been keeping an eye out for messages on church signs and writing them down. And special thanks goes to Pastor Curry Pikkaart, a local pastor who has shared with me his collection of more than two hundred captions, and to Marjorie Carlisle, whose captions at the Pleasant View Church of Christ near Cassopolis, Michigan, have inspired me and who sent me about a hundred from her collection.

Finally, I want to give a word of thanks to Jim Ruark, fellow senior editor at Zondervan, who saw the vision of this book and brought it through the editorial process and various marketing meetings to its present form. And to the members of the ARMoR marketing team, also a hearty thank you for all you've done.

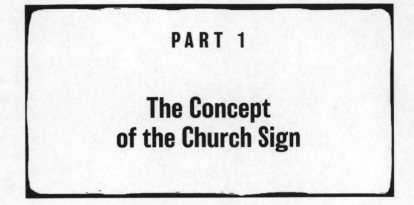

PART 1

The Concept
of the Church Sign

CHAPTER 1

The Purpose of the Church Sign

For most, if not all, of the twentieth century, churches have proudly indicated who they were by the use of specially built signs, often standing a few feet in front of and off to the side of their front doors. As automobiles became more and more popular, the sign moved to a place where it would be visible to passing vehicles, even if the church itself was set much farther from the road. At the beginning, the sign was generally used to indicate the name of the church, the time of its worship services and Sunday school, and sometimes the name of its pastor. More recently, as we will see, churches have found more creative uses for their signs.

The Advertising Philosophy of Outdoor Signs

The church sign falls within the area of promotion known as outdoor advertising.[1] Included in this field of advertising are billboards, posters, and transit advertising (e.g., the signs on buses). The main goal of outdoor advertising is to reach people traveling by in their vehicles quickly with a catchy message that they will remember. "The job of the billboard is to create a quick impression and to remind a viewer that a product, a service, or a nearby business exists."[2]

In general, the maximum amount of time an advertiser has to communicate a message is seven seconds. But since drivers need to keep their eyes attuned to other traffic, for the majority of cars (those without passengers) the time allotted is more likely between three and five seconds. Only if traffic happens to be stalled or if a sign is visible to cars stopped at a traffic signal will

---

[1]Two good books that discuss the use of outdoor advertising are Otto Kleppner, *Advertising Procedure,* 5th ed. (Englewood Cliffs, N.J.: Prentice-Hall, 1995), 207–19; Jeanette Smith, *The Advertising Kit: A Complete Guide for Small Businesses* (New York: Macmillan, 1994), 207–18.

[2]Smith, *The Advertising Kit,* 208.

a business get longer than a few seconds of examination by a potential consumer. Obviously, therefore, anything an advertiser wants to communicate has to be done with a minimum number of words. If the message can be communicated by a picture, so much the better; in advertising the adage is indeed true: A picture is worth a thousand words. If the sign is lighted, its value increases, for then advertising can occur twenty-four hours a day rather than just during the daylight hours.

Another important issue concerning the billboard is the angle at which the sign is placed to the road. In most cases, the sign should be placed at right angles to the road or perhaps at sixty degrees; this allows the maximum amount of time to digest the sign's message. True, a sign placed parallel to a road can be read by traffic going in both directions, but in general the amount of time those in a vehicle have to read what the sign says (if they even see it) drops to a maximum of two seconds. Usually signs that are parallel to the road simply indicate the business located on a particular piece of property.

Another truism concerning outdoor advertising is that "familiarity breeds contempt." That is, the more often one drives by a certain sign that remains the same, the less one sees it or remembers it. Just as you become immune to hearing a clock in your house chime every fifteen minutes (though visitors always notice), you also become immune to the message on a sign that never changes. This is one of the main reasons why billboard space is sold by the month or at the most three months; after that, its advertising value decreases unless the message is changed or moved to a new location.

The Church Sign

How do these principles of the outdoor sign apply to the church sign? Few churches advertise via the billboard. Such advertising is expensive (especially if the sign is in a prime location), and there is no good mechanism to figure out a "return on the investment." Rather, most church signs are located somewhere on church property, usually at a place where they are visible to people driving by. Local zoning ordinances in most cases regulate the size of signs—often they are allowed to be not much larger than a standard sheet of plywood. Thus, with a permanent location and a relatively small size, a sign's chances of being noticed on a regular basis decrease significantly.

Most church leaders want people to become aware of the name and location of their church. People who offer advice on where churches should be located suggest streets that have a relatively high volume of traffic. Unless the congregation has an aggressive evangelism program, a church building located on a cul-de-sac has little opportunity of attracting visitors except from that particular neighborhood plat and from people who are loyal to its specific denomination. Only if the church has something like a high steeple visible to vehicles driving on a main artery will casual passersby even become aware of its existence. A few towns and cities do permit signs several blocks away, pointing to the church and identifying it.

Obviously, the busier the street on which a church is located, the more likely it is to be noticed. It is important for a church sign to be placed at right angles to the street. Recently I was talking with a colleague at work, who mentioned that she attended Church A. "Oh," I replied, "the church on Street X close to the bridge?"

"No," she responded. "That's Church B. This one is Street Y." Now, I drive down both streets X and Y two or three times a week, and for some reason I had only a vague idea of where Church A was. The next time I drove that route, I looked for it, and sure enough, there it was. Guess what? Its sign was parallel to the road, whereas Church B had a sign that was at right angles.

In addition, be sure that the sign is as close to the road as local laws will allow. I have been trying to read the caption on one church I go past regularly, but I usually cannot since it is about fifty feet back from the road. If I cannot read it, what about people who aren't looking for the caption?

But even if the church sign is at right angles to the road, there still is the problem of its familiarity. For people traveling that same road every day, the sign becomes part of the landscape, seen only in the periphery of one's vision but not really noticed. How can a church continue to draw attention to its existence at that location? The best way—and perhaps the only way—is by having a sign that allows for movable type to be placed on it.

Using movable type on a church sign, of course, is nothing new. My father was the pastor of a small-town church in northwest Washington in the early 1950s. The church he served was located on the main street of the town, and the church had a sign (parallel to the street) that allowed for movable type. Each Friday either he or the custodian would place the sermon titles for the morning and afternoon service on the sign. I am not sure whether the church board ever questioned what "advertising" function this pattern served. Perhaps it was to pique the interest of passersby in the sermon topics and so perhaps draw in visitors. But in a town that was highly churched, this was really not much of an option. By and large, it served to give the parishioners an advance on the information they would read Sunday in the weekly bulletin.

The Functions of Movable Type Signs

Church signs with movable type, however, can serve several other functions, both of an advertising and of an evangelistic type. This is especially the case if the captions put on the church sign are designed to catch the attention of people driving by.

1. One important function has already been hinted at. If the caption on the church sign is changed consistently, those who drive by regularly see the sign afresh each time. In fact, it can even be something that drivers look forward to in order to break the monotony of their morning or evening commute.

Let me illustrate. For several years I commuted from Michigan to Indiana to attend graduate school at the University of Notre Dame. As I turned on to Michigan Highway 60 at Three Rivers and approached Cassopolis, I regularly drove past the Pleasant View Church of Christ, which had displayed a portable, lighted, yellow marquee (which has subsequently been replaced by a classier-looking, built-in sign). Every two or three weeks the saying on the sign changed, and I always looked forward to seeing what the new caption was. I can picture exactly where this church is located—a church I might easily have missed were it not for that sign. Marjorie Carlisle, an elderly woman who has managed that sign for years, wrote to me that the church has received numerous comments and letters about their church sign. One person even stopped at the parsonage and left a gift of twenty dollars toward its upkeep!

I recently read an e-mail from Pastor Kip Hoech of Our Savior's Community Church in Palm Springs, California. He wrote that they change their sign about twice a week. Part of the time, of course, they use it to publicize church events or activities of general interest to the public. But usually it has catchy captions on it, designed to make people think. People notice the sign. Pastor Hoech has been told of several people who have changed their route to the supermarket just to read the church sign. Now that's being visible!

2. The caption on a church sign can also serve as an identity marker. Again let me illustrate. Before I moved to Grand Rapids, Michigan, I was aware that this city had a drive-in church that met for worship at a local drive-in theater. I must admit, I wondered what type of an outfit this was and what type of messages were preached there. Did they promote a generic "God loves everyone" theology? Was the sermon focused on "the power of positive thinking"? Or did those who preached there testify to the evangelical message of salvation in Jesus Christ alone? After I became the pastor of this Woodland Drive-In Church, I knew that this last option characterized its preaching. I also realized that the church is a ministry outreach of Fifth Reformed Church in Grand Rapids, which adheres to all the essentials of the evangelical Christian faith.[3]

But how would other people know that unless they actually attended one of our services? And how would they know in advance what kind of message they would hear? In many cases, people want to know at least something about a church before they begin to attend. A denominational affiliation, of course, is a good indication of where a church stands theologically. But the Task Force of the Woodland Drive-In Church decided long ago not to advertise openly who were its sponsors. Thus, when we

---

[3]You can find out more about this church at www.driveinchurch.org.

moved from the Woodland Drive-In Theater to our new, permanent location after the drive-in theater closed, we set up a church sign that allows for movable type. By reading the changing captions that are put on the sign, one gets a fairly good idea of who we are and what we stand for.

3. A third function for a changeable sign is to announce significant events that will occur in the church. If you have a major anniversary celebration, by all means advertise it on your church sign. Advertisement for your Daily Vacation Bible School also belongs on that sign. Or if you are having a special event, such as a special concert or a community outreach program—or even a soup supper—let people driving by know about it. You can never tell who might want to attend that event, yet would not be attending, were it not for the sign.

4. A final function for changeable captions on a church sign is to trigger helpful and inspiring thoughts in the minds and hearts of those driving by. Even if people never attend your particular church, you can bless them with insights for everyday living as they drive to and from work or shopping malls. Captions can remind them of the importance of praying, attending church, accepting Jesus as their personal Savior, seeing God's will in everything that happens, finding encouragement for struggles they are going through, and so forth. Especially if the caption has a clever twist to it, it can stick with an individual for a long time. You may never know how many people your sign ministry has blessed, but the Lord does, and that is what counts.

CHAPTER 2

The Caption

Since the wording is so important if one is to use the church sign as a means of advertising, identity, and outreach, we should explore various aspects of the caption. The main purpose of this book is to give you more than one thousand suggestions on captions that you can use for your own church sign.

Size and Length

Church sign captions must be brief and to the point. Ten to twelve words is the maximum that should be placed on a sign. People traveling by at thirty to forty miles per hour and trying to pay attention to other vehicles on the road have very little time to read a message. If you are fortunate enough, as we at the Woodland Drive-In Church are, to have your sign on a corner that has a traffic light, people will have more time to digest its message. But by and large you should plan a caption that is geared for people traveling by without stopping.

Personally, I think it is ideal to have at least three lines on which to put letters. (We have only two, and that severely limits the type and length of the message we can put on.) If you go to four lines, the tendency is to put on more than the maximum number of words; moreover, people have greater difficulty reading both horizontally and vertically. A narrow sign with four or five lines, however, is just fine.

It is also important to have sufficient spaces between words—the wider, the better. Whenever I have had to put five or more words on a line, I am sure that people miss the message the first time they see it because the words are simply too close together. Only if they really want to read the caption and look at it more than once will they get what it says.

Some of the captions included in the following lists will not fit easily on two-line signs (depending on the size of your letters), but

I have included them anyway. You may have to be creative in editing and adjusting a message. For example, one caption reads: "You cannot stumble when you are on your knees." This caption has nine simple words and thirty-seven characters (not including spaces), but I found it impossible to put it on our two-line sign without virtually eliminating all spaces between the words. Thus I edited it to read: "You can't stumble while on your knees"— seven words and thirty-one characters. It says essentially the same thing and fits nicely on our sign.

Even longer sayings can be edited down to fit, with a bit of creativity. One of the captions included in this book reads: "When you are reluctant to change, think of the beauty of autumn." It contains twelve words and sixty-three characters, far more than what our sign could handle. I revised it to read: "Reluctant to change? Think of fall's beauty"—seven words and thirty-seven characters (several of them being narrow characters). With this editing, I was able to fit it on our sign.

Speaking of characters, I do need to point out that character count is not everything. Also important is what characters of the alphabet or number system you use. In the space of one *M,* for example, you can put three or four *I*'s. In our sign font, many of the letters vary significantly in size.

Accuracy

One of the most important elements of a sign is its accuracy— both spelling and grammar. The greatest nightmare of anyone responsible for putting up a sign caption is that he or she will spell a word incorrectly. Check and recheck the spelling, both as you plan the caption and after you have put it on the sign. Grammar can be equally important. The only time I was specifically complimented on a sign caption came when a woman told me she was pleased that I had used correct grammar. The caption she was referring to was the following: "Consider whom you serve, not what you have." Had I used the wording "who you serve," most people may not have caught the error, but it was important to at least one person, and grammar shows an attention to detail.

I also advise having an adequate set of punctuation marks for your sign. It is true that you can probably get away with putting a question on a sign and not have it end with a question mark, but the sign looks so much better if it does. We have question marks, periods, semi colons, exclamation marks, commas, apostrophes, and quotation marks—all of which we have used at one time or another. I wish we had dashes and hyphens, but we don't. Punctuation marks can also aid in shortening captions if you have only two lines to work with. For example, one caption reads: "Life is a puzzle. Look here for the missing peace"—nine words and forty characters. With a question mark I was able to shorten it to this: "Life's a puzzle? Look here for missing peace"—eight words and thirty-seven characters. Tight, but it did work. In fact, almost any "if" or "when" clause can be shortened by changing it to a question.

Types of Captions

A wide variety of captions can be used on church signs and are included in this book. One of the most traditional, of course, is to use Scripture. It is never inappropriate to have on your sign Acts 16:31: "Believe in the Lord Jesus Christ, and you will be saved." Or to use Luke 2:11 during the Christmas season: "Unto you is born this day a Savior, Christ the Lord" (paraphrased). I do not include many Scripture captions in this book, since I assume you are creative enough to find your own. If you do use such captions and you have room to cite the biblical book-chapter-verse reference, I suggest you do so. Anything we can do to improve people's Bible knowledge and make them aware of its relevance is laudable.

Seasonal captions are always appropriate—Advent, Christmas, Lent, Easter, Memorial Day, Fourth of July, Labor Day, Thanksgiving Day, and so on. The most important thing about such captions is that they should be changed soon after the season or holiday is over. Keeping a Christmas caption up well into January, even if the weather is cold, shows a certain carelessness or inattention that does not bode well for your church.

The most effective signs involve a play on words. After all, a sign caption is composed of words; that's all we have to work with.

The pun is thus one of the favorite ways to communicate a message. Sometimes the play on words can come because of English homonyms: "We have a prophet-sharing plan." This type of word-play can even be based on the sounds of letters rather than on specific words; a common caption is "CH CH. What's missing? UR." It may take people a minute or so to catch the meaning of such a caption, but that's okay—you have gotten their attention.

A caption can also play on two meanings for the same word or phrase: "Home improvement: Take your family to church." Sometimes the play on words is not exactly right, but close enough to make clear what is going on: "Come in for a faith lift." Another good way to get a message across is by playing on opposites: "Give God what is right, not what is left" or "God often uses a setback to move us ahead."

Obviously, humor is also a clever way to get your sign noticed. One of the most interesting ones I have recently seen reads this way: "Sign broken. Message inside." That church was trying to get people to attend their worship services. A humorous one in a different vein is "God's gonna toot; we're gonna scoot"—reminding people of the return of Jesus Christ at the sound of the trumpet. One ought to be careful, however, not to get too cutesy in the humor, or crass. We do not want to give the appearance of being flippant about our faith.

Another good design for a caption is to use a metaphor—a truth in nature, for example, that carries a corresponding spiritual message. For a metaphor to work, of course, it has to be obvious to the reader in few words and without any accompanying explanation. For example, in the caption "Fog, clouds, and rain help land stay lush with greenery," the message is that just as cloudy and rainy days are needed for living things to blossom forth in beauty, so times of trouble and darkness often result in spiritual blessing and fruit in our lives. Or again, the caption "Forcing a rosebud open ruins the flower" communicates that if we run ahead of God's will and try to force his hand, we are following a recipe for disaster; many experiences in life take time, and it is always best to follow God's timing. Many of the captions included in this book contain metaphors.

What about allusions to Scripture? Given what we read about the woeful lack of basic Bible knowledge today, I tend to shy away from such captions. For example, you might put on the caption, "In the storms of life, hear Jesus say, Peace, be still!" This is an obvious allusion to the story in Mark 4:35–41 about Jesus' stilling of the storm on the Sea of Galilee, when the disciples were terrified and cried out to him for help. But would those who pass by your sign catch the allusion? Some undoubtedly would, and you may wish to use this one and develop others like it. Personally, however, I think the vast majority of people, except in well-churched areas, would not know that you are alluding to the Bible in that caption. (Yet that particular caption does have value even for those who don't know the Bible story.)

The adaptation of current slogans, common secular proverbs, and even parts of popular songs is also a fruitful source for pithy church sign captions. Recently I put this caption on our sign: "T G I F—Thank God I'm forgiven." Slogans and hit songs keep changing, of course, so you need to keep your ear attuned to what is current. You should probably not use a caption of this nature after it has run its course. A good example of adapting a slogan might be "God cared enough to send his very best"—an obvious take-off on the Hallmark theme. Or, during the summer months when people go on vacation, try this one: "God: Don't leave home without him"—an adaptation of a popular American Express slogan. One advantage of using these sorts of captions is that you can multiply their effect. The next time a person hears the original caption—let's say in a commercial—his or her mind may easily go back to your sign and its message.

Also useful, I think, are Christian children's songs. There are many people (especially among the so-called Baby Boomers) who went to church and Sunday school in their childhood, though they have long since stopped. They sang songs like "Jesus Loves Me" and probably still know some of them by heart. Putting a song like that on a sign might trigger a long-lost memory, especially if the person reading it is going through a difficult time. I can imagine a man in his forties, struggling with a difficult home or work situation, singing that song on the way to work after seeing your sign—at least singing it in his mind. Obviously, the entire song cannot go on a sign at one time, but it might even work to mount, on successive weeks, the four lines of the first verse of that song plus the chorus (the part everyone remembers).

Themes of Captions

Captions for signs can take a wide variety of themes, but all of them, in one way or another, are designed to get people to think. During specific seasons, the intent is to get people to think of the real meaning for that particular season rather than what society has done to secularize it. And in the rush of everyday life, it is always appropriate to get people to think about what is really important—the Lord Jesus Christ and the fact of an eternity that is awaiting us. Material goods have little of eternal significance to offer; what really counts is our relationship to God.

One of the most powerful themes of captions is encouragement to people going through crises in their lives, and we all face crises at one time or another. Thus a number of the captions I have included in this book stress that bringing our needs to the Lord in prayer is important, that God is in charge of our lives and will work all things for our good, and that the goal of the church is to help people cope with struggles in life and to offer certainty for the ultimate aim of life—spending eternity with Jesus.

Finally, it is occasionally appropriate to have captions that deal with important personal and social issues apart from any overtly religious content. Note how much of the book of Proverbs contains two-liners with such messages. Marriages, for example, are often in trouble today, and spouses may not know how to communicate. Fathers and mothers struggle with parenting issues. The country as a whole could stand for a good dose of public morality. Therefore captions that address issues such as these can be helpful to people even though they may not be believers. Let's face it: The most important attitude we can have in life and all its relationships—and the one we least often express—is unconditional love.

I would issue two cautions, however, regarding the use of captions that have a more generic flavor. First, I suggest you shy away from political issues, partly because these can offend people (the last thing you want to do with your sign) and partly because they brand your church politically, not doctrinally. Second, I suggest these sorts of captions be used less rather than more frequently, since citing psychological and social truisms will not help identify the evangelical message that God has given to the church to proclaim. If your caption could be put on the sign of the most liberal church in town or even on a McDonald's sign, you have not witnessed to the saving message of God's Word.

Remember, when all is said and done, the caption you put on your sign is a mini-sermon to the world around you. Let it say what you want the world to hear.

PART 2

Captions for the Church Sign

Introduction

The captions listed in the rest of this book have been divided up into different categories. I begin with seasonal captions (going from January to December). That unit is followed by captions according to specific themes such as prayer, encouragement, God in charge, or living the Christian life. The last few sections have generic captions—messages that are not unique to Christianity but are certainly compatible with the Christian life.

Please note that many captions can fit more than one category. That is certainly the case for the seasonal captions; some of them, in fact, can be used at almost any time. Also, I could easily have scattered the captions that are adaptations of slogans and familiar sayings throughout the other sections, but I felt it best to provide them as a separate unit.

Many of the captions are somewhat lengthy—far more than what can be read easily in just a couple seconds by people driving by. But many churches are located on street corners by stop signs or traffic signals, and people welcome the time to divert their attention to reading something worthwhile. Also, if your church sign is in a twenty-five-mile-per-hour zone, the amount of time for reading a caption increases. In fact, in most urban places, what limits the size of the caption is not the speed of the traffic but the size of the sign.

As I indicated earlier, feel free to adapt these captions to your own particular need. And if you have a smaller sign, just use the smaller captions. You will generally be able to figure out what size caption fits on your sign by how far it goes across the page. Once you know which size fits the maximum, you may wish to draw a light penciled line on each page, knowing that any caption to the left of that line fits comfortably and any that extend past it to the right will need adaptation.

Space is provided beneath each caption either to put a date when you use it or to write any adaptation you use.

NEW YEAR'S DAY

God can make all things new, even you

Life offers changes; God offers a new life

Resolve to let God solve your problems

Let your resolution be his solution

Resolution for [*year*]: To know Jesus better

On the threshold of a New Year, let God hold you

Better than counting your years is to make all your
years count

Jesus adds life to your years and years to your life

May all your troubles be as short as your New Year's
resolutions

VALENTINE'S DAY

The way to God begins with a broken heart

To love God is to know him

Jesus' Valentine message: Yours forever

God loves you, whether you like it or not

People are at the heart of God's heart

SPRING

It takes time and rain to create rainbows

The fruitful life seeks rain as well as sunshine

Dark clouds bring showers of blessing

A contrary wind raises the kite higher

It wasn't raining when Noah built the ark

The beauty in nature is God's greeting card

Spring is God's way of saying "One more time"

The birds are back, the grass is green; God did it again!

Does your spiritual house need a spring cleaning?

Spring into life with Jesus

Pray for a good harvest, but keep on plowing

LENT

T G G F—Thank God for Good Friday

Beat the Easter rush, come to church this Sunday

Leave your sorrows to the "Man of Sorrows"

Jesus: The light of the world hung in darkness

Jesus' love, not human nails, held him to the cross

Calvary is proof that sin troubled God; does it trouble you?

The victim of Good Friday is the victor of Easter

Christ crossed out our sins on Calvary

Human unrighteousness has brought about God's
   righteousness

EASTER

Easter—the rest of the Christmas story

The Easter story is not a dead issue

Jesus changes grave situation; happy Easter!

We are Easter people living in a Good Friday world

Where do you fit in the Easter story?

Only a risen Savior can save a dying world

Easter moves our thoughts from death to life

Christ's empty tomb guarantees our victory over death

News flash: A tomb in Jerusalem is empty! ~2007

The best argument for a risen Christ is a living Christian

Emphasize the Easter heart, not the Easter hat

The Gospels don't explain the resurrection; the
   resurrection explains the Gospel

MOTHER'S DAY AND FATHER'S DAY

Nobody is poor who has had a godly mother

If God is your Father, the church is your mother

Children of God, obey your Father

Those born of God should resemble their Father

Good fathers/mothers don't just give life; they teach how to live

A father/mother is someone you look up to, no matter how tall you grow

PENTECOST

Spirit of the living God, fall fresh on me!

Lonely? God has sent his Holy Comforter

Overwhelmed? God has sent his Holy Helper

Confused? God has sent his Holy Counselor

Let the anointing oil of God's Spirit reduce your friction

To understand the Word of God, rely on the Spirit of God

MEMORIAL DAY (OR ARMISTICE DAY)

Love is stronger than death

I will remember the goodness of God

SUMMER

This church is prayer conditioned

Dry spells cause roots to go deep

Deep roots give strength in times of storm

Fog, clouds, and rain help land stay lush with greenery

Bask in the warmth of God's Son

Tend your heart well; it is God's garden

The garden of life requires regular cultivation

Remember three gardens: Eden, Gethsemane, Paradise

Thank God not only for the roses but also for the thorns

If you think it's hot here. . .

Summer: A great time for personal re-creation

God never goes on vacation from you

FOURTH OF JULY
(OR ANY NATIONAL HOLIDAY)

Remember that American ends with I can

Only one bound to Christ is truly free

Our greatest freedom is freedom from sin

A nation is only as strong as the character of its citizens

The church: Band of the free, home of the saved

Our citizenship in heaven defines our duties on earth

To be truly free, work for the freedom of others

Liberty is genuine only if you give it to others

Some pursue happiness; others create it

The best way to change this country is to change yourself

"In God we trust": Right on the money

Christ shall have dominion from sea to sea
   [for Dominion Day in Canada]

LABOR DAY

Work for the night is coming

Have your tools ready and God will find you work

All Christians work for the same employer

Life works better when we do

Work becomes worship when done for the Lord

Workers are more important to God than the work

School: A place with four walls and tomorrow inside

FALL

Live within your harvest

Pray for a good harvest, but continue to hoe

Suffering is God's tool to plow the ground for greater harvest

An abundant harvest requires much weeding and pruning

When you are reluctant to change, think of the beauty of autumn

Winter is coming, so is the Lord: Are you prepared?

HALLOWEEN

No mask will ever hide your sin from God

Make every evening a hallowed evening

Beware! The devil masquerades as an angel of light

God sets us free from the need to wear masks

Don't fear ghosts; believe in the Holy Ghost

THANKSGIVING DAY

Faith flourishes in the garden of gratitude

Thankfulness is the soil in which joy thrives

A grateful mind is a great mind

Gratitude is a God-honoring attitude

Those who are thankful for little enjoy much

Real thanksgiving is thanksliving

We don't need more to be thankful for, we need to be
more thankful

ADVENT AND CHRISTMAS

Christ is the biggest part of Christmas

Wise men still seek him; so do wise women

Unto you is born this day a Savior

Empty cradle? Empty Christmas

Without Christmas there would be no Easter

Born in a manger, now preparing us a mansion

Celebrate God's great Christmas gift—salvation

We can come to Jesus because Jesus came to us

Jesus came to earth to take us to heaven

The world's best gift was wrapped in a manger

Peace begins not at a Mideast table but at a Mideast stable

Christmas in the heart puts Christmas in the air

The shepherds heard an angel and found their Lamb

Jesus Christ is a gift to be shared

Jesus was born that we might be born again

Santa offers ho, ho, ho; Jesus offers health, help, and hope

WINTER

After the cold winter, roses will bloom again

The cold world needs warm-hearted Christians

If the world seems cold, kindle the warming fires of love

Don't be snowed under by sin; turn to Jesus

Adaptations of Proverbs, Slogans, Sayings, and Songs

God cared enough to send his very best

God: Don't leave home without him

Salvation: Don't leave life without it

T G I F—Thank God I'm forgiven

Did somebody say salvation?

Wal-Mart is not the only savings place

God is like Coca-Cola; he's the real thing

God gets the stains out that others leave behind

Jesus will do it all for you

We can have our best witness in the worst of times

Jesus Christ: Like a rock

There are some things money can't buy—like salvation

It's not over until Jesus returns

Grace happens

Take me up, Jesus

W W J D?

Get in line with God: www.bible.god

Believe in Jesus; just do it!

Have it God's way

God is up to something good

Big brother Jesus is watching you

No one chills out in the fires of hell

If you can't stand the heat, believe in Jesus

Salvation: It does a person good

Got Jesus?

Put on Jesus as the fabric of your life

Heaven: The place where God knows your name

No fear! No fear? Fear God!

Give sin an inch and it will take a mile

To be or not to be saved; that is the question

All's well that ends in heaven

The best laid plans begin with God

Count to ten, and remember God loves you

On your mark, get set, go—with God

The Bible: Breakfast of spiritual champions

Jesus loves me, this I know; for the Bible tells me so

The wise man built his house upon a rock

Christian love means having to say "I'm sorry"

"I shall return!" Said by Jesus Christ

Be all you can be, with the help of God's Spirit

Lord, make me an instrument of your peace

The pilot of the universe never commits error

If God is your copilot, better change seats

There may be no free lunches, but salvation is free

Jesus and salvation: You can't have one without the other

Have a great day, and have it with Christ

Just say "Yes" to Jesus

God is a promise keeper

I love what you do for me, dear Jesus

Give me a break, God. "OK, believe in my Son Jesus"

The 3 R's: Repentance, Receiving Christ, Redemption

God's Word: The truth, the whole truth, and nothing but
the truth

"Not good if detached" is also true of church members

Jesus is my rock; my name is on his roll

Captions on Marriage and the Family

Husband, wife, God: A three-strand cord is not
easily broken

"Loved the wedding, invite me to the marriage." God

A good marriage is the union of two forgivers

Fewer marriages would fail if those who said "I do" did

Many people spend more time preparing for a wedding
than for a marriage

Some people change mates but never think of changing
themselves

Put Christ first if you want your marriage to last

If grass looks greener on the other side, fertilize yours

Children need models, not critics

Children need your time, not your money

Little children are a big concern to Jesus

The best inheritance to leave your children is a
    good example

As the twig is bent, so grows the tree

Children: Today's investment, tomorrow's dividend

Invest in the future: Lead a child to Christ

First talk to God about your children, then to your
    children about God

Parents are just baby-sitters for God

Be the soul support of [or provider for] your children

Don't let your parents down; they brought you up

Do you really want your children to grow up to be
    just like you?

The family that prays together stays together

A family altar will alter many a family

Captions Related to Prayer

Feeling let down today? Try looking up

When life gets you down, take time to look up

It's looking down that makes one dizzy

When you are swept off your feet, slip down on your knees

Kneeling keeps you in good standing with God

Those who stand best kneel most

If you kneel before God, you can stand up for anything

If your trouble is deep-seated and long-standing,
   try kneeling

Don't let adversity get you down except on your knees

Backsliding begins when knee-bending stops

If you can't sleep, don't count sheep, talk to the Shepherd

You can't stumble when you are on your knees

You learn to walk by starting on your knees

When life knocks you on your knees, pray there

Improve your outlook by looking up

A prayer is a wish turned heavenward

The secret to praying is praying in secret

Prayer doesn't need proof, it needs practice

Praying is talking to our best Friend

God is never too busy to listen to his children

God answers prayer with yes, no, or wait

Seven days without prayer makes one weak

A day hemmed with prayer is less likely to unravel

Give your troubles to God; he's up all night anyway

When life is hard, pray harder

Pray hardest when it is hardest to pray

Sorrow looks back, worry looks around, faith looks up

Turn life's cares into prayers

You never get a busy signal on the line to heaven

True prayer is a way of life, not an emergency

Strength in prayer is better than length in prayer

You do not need many words to open your heart to God

The best way to remember people is in prayer

Daily prayers lessen daily cares

Face each day with the face of God

"We need to talk." God

Why worry when you can pray?

To make the most of your time, take time to pray

God is not afraid of your questions

Express your feelings to God; he can handle them

God may let us struggle until we ask for help

Prayer changes the way we look at the world around us

Praying is as easy as talking with a friend

Because God is everywhere, you can pray anywhere

No matter how far you've run away from God, he's only a
    prayer away

Nothing is too great or too small to bring to God

Prayerless pews make powerless pulpits

Courage is fear that has said its prayers

Life is fragile; handle with prayer

Get an expert opinion; pray to God

If you pray as you ought, you will live as you pray

To pray in the hard times, learn to pray in the easy times

Never pray in a way that diminishes your faith

Ask God to close every door but the right one

O God, take me, break me, make me

Not expecting answers from God wastes his time
    and yours

A life without prayer is a powerless life

Prayer is the key of the day and the lock of the night

If you have no time to pray, you become easy prey

If God feels far away, he's not the one who moved

Prayer is one weapon the enemy cannot copy
    [or duplicate]

You may not move things on earth with your prayers
    [or with prayer], but you may move heaven

Don't pray for tasks equal to your power; pray for power
    equal to your tasks

A single thought raised to God is a perfect prayer

Thank God for dirty dishes; at least you have food

God, I need faith to move not a mountain, but to move me

God has an 800 number: Prayer

Praying will give you a calm-plex

Let prayer be the mortar that holds your life together

Captions of Encouragement

Faith grows stronger as we climb higher

Faith keeps the person who keeps the faith

Faith turns sealed caves into tunnels

Faith removes mountains or tunnels through

When doubts arise, faith builds skyscrapers

Faith is a gift, but you have to ask for it

Jesus cares

"I love you and you and you and ..." God

Worry not who you are but Whose you are

Christians never see the last of each other

Good-byes are the law of earth, reunions the law of heaven

God loves each one as if there is but one to love

Faith in Jesus is the believer's passport to heaven

To withstand temptation, stand with Christ

Earth has no sorrow that heaven does not feel

Earth has no sorrow that heaven cannot heal

God may break us in order to remake us

Faith focuses on God instead of the problem

The beginning of true faith is the end of anxiety

Patience is trusting in God's timing

Trust yourself less and God more

Exercise your faith; walk with God

It's always darkest just before dawn

In a tunnel of discouragement, walk toward the light

In the dark? Look to God for light

In the dark? Jesus is the light of the world

Experts made the Titanic; amateurs made the ark

Smooth seas don't make skillful sailors

No sailor ever reached the destination by staying
in the harbor

No trial is without God's blessing

No burden is too heavy for the everlasting arms

Count your blessings, not your burdens

If God places a burden on you, he places his arms
underneath you

Can't sleep? Count your blessings, not sheep

Fear is unbelief in disguise

Be still and know that I am God

Impatience is a form of unbelief

A diamond cannot be shaped without friction

Diamonds are formed from coal that outlasted the
    pressure on them

Faith can never overdraw its account in God's bank

Death is not a dead end but a fork in the road

Let hope of Christ's coming keep you going

God always performs what he promises

God will not say "No" to something he has promised

Step out in faith on the promises of God

Don't carry tomorrow's burdens with today's grace

To see beyond earth's shadows, look to Christ the light

Shadows fall behind when we walk toward the light

Trusting in God can turn a trial into a triumph

Trusting God can transform a trial into a treasure

God gives special grace for each trial we face

Christ behind you, Christ beside you, Christ before you

God holds our heads higher than the deepest waters

Smile! God loves you

Let God unravel the tangles of your life

Release the past; enjoy the present; embrace the future

It is wise to walk with someone who knows the way
    (John 14:6)

Let Jesus calm your troubled waters

You can feel safe in your Father's arms

God made each of us different but loves all of us the same

Wherever I go, there "I am"

Trying times are not the time to stop trying

Joy is often the inner lining of suffering

With Christ in our hearts, we are never alone

It's easy to be an angel if no one ruffles your feathers

It takes a storm to prove life's real shelter

With Jesus' help, turn a crucifixion into a resurrection

Pain is no evil unless it conquers us

The first step to victory: Know the enemy

To realize the value of an anchor, we need to feel a storm

Feed your faith and your fears [*or* doubts] will starve
    to death

Faith isn't a leap in the dark but a step into light

Peace is the surest sign of God's presence

In life's battles, put God between yourself and your enemy

Jesus never asks us to enter a valley he has not passed
    through

You cannot enjoy victory until you have fought the battle

Resisting temptation doubles spiritual strength

Faith that goes forward triumphs

Look to eternity when the present collapses around you

Life's trials are God's school of faith

With God in the soul's center there is peace

Evil never surrenders its grasp without a fight

Genuine faith puts a letter in the mailbox and lets go

Remember: God has not yet finished making you

Dark days are stepping stones on the path to light

Walking with God in the dark is better than walking alone
    in the light

Forcing a rosebud open spoils the flower

Sing, don't reason, your worries away

God reserves his best medicine for our times of deepest
    despair

Beneath the pounding rain are growing spiritual flowers

If you are at the end of your rope, ask God to tie a knot

If you feel at loose ends, ask God to tie a knot

It doesn't take a lot of muscle to give the heart a lift

We cannot direct the winds, but we can adjust the sails

If you don't climb the mountain, you can't see the view

Carve your stumbling blocks into stepping stones

A sturdy oak isn't grown in a greenhouse

If you can't see the bright side, polish the dull side

Ironing out problems without Jesus puts wrinkles on
your face

A head hung in despair cannot scan the horizon of God's
provision

Earth's best does not compare with heaven's least

When we do what we can, God will do what we can't

There is no pit so deep that Jesus is not deeper still

Christ turns sunsets into dawns

I have a great need for Christ; I have a great Christ for
my need

God doesn't need great men; great men need God

Captions of Going to Church

Sign broken; come inside for message

Thirsty and hungry? Come to church

Home improvement: Take your family to church

Visitors aren't just welcome; they're expected

Tough week? We're open Sunday

Heaven knows when you were here last

CH CH What's missing? UR

Come in for a faith lift

A half-hour of preaching is like raising the dead

We welcome you with open Psalms

Don't drive by; drive in [*this one is especially suitable for a drive-in church*]

Life is a puzzle; look here for the missing peace

Churches are yours, attend one

Come in and let us prepare you for your finals

"C'mon over and bring the kids." God

There are many ways to worship God, but only one God
    to worship

Don't wait for the hearse to take you to church

We have a prophet-sharing plan

Try our Sundays; they are better than Baskin Robbins

For a special treat, try one of our Sundays

We help people glow, grow, and go

This church is a hospital for sinners, not a museum
    for saints

Come worship in the Sonshine

Hear God's Word here

You aren't too bad to come in; you aren't too good to
    stay out

Interested in going to heaven? Apply here for flight
    training

Free trip to heaven; details inside

Sunday is the golden clasp that binds together the volume
    of the week

The surest steps toward happiness are the church steps

Vacancy: Every Sunday, 11 A.M.

All of our seats come with a first class service

Soular-powered by the Son

Wanted: Imperfect people

See U in S NDAY SCHOOL

Evangelistic Captions

CAPTIONS WITH AN
EVANGELISTIC MESSAGE

God likes people—he sent his Son to be one!

Our salvation is free because Christ paid the price

To live without God means to die without hope

To have a fulfilled life, let God fill you

Now is the time to invest in eternity

It's never too soon [*or* too late] to plan for eternity

"Will the road you're on get you to my place?" God

"Do you have any idea where you're going?" God

To know happiness, get to know Jesus

Christ believed is salvation received

No God, no peace; know God, know peace

God's mercy is greater than your greatest sin

God can't find us if we don't know we're lost

We are never so lost that God can't find us

Short on time? How about eternal life?

GRACE: God's Riches At Christ's Expense

Only one road leads to heaven

To make something of life, give your life to God

To renew your love for God, review God's love for you

Salvation is what we receive, not what we achieve

Check up before you check out

Get a life! Believe in Jesus

Life with Christ is endless hope; life without Christ is
    a hopeless end

Christ is not valued at all unless he is valued above all

Christians never meet for the last time

If being born hasn't brought happiness, be born again

Heaven: Don't miss it for the world

No one ever regretted Christianity on a deathbed

Is your passport for eternity in order?

To be heaven bound, you must be heaven born

Do you manage, or does he?

The wages of sin have never been reduced

Almost saved is not good enough

A child of God is always welcomed home

Many children are afraid of the dark; many adults are
    afraid of the light

Give your all to him who gave his all for you

Refusing Jesus is a no-win situation

Life is a gift from God to be given back to him

Our salvation was costly to God but it is free to us

What we do after here determines where we go hereafter

Heaven: No pain, all gain

Not to decide for Christ is a decision

God always gives us another chance on earth

God has no lottery system for entering heaven

Jesus is your only life assurance policy

If you don't have Jesus, you don't have anything

It's not where we begin but where we end that matters

Where will you be spending eternity—smoking or
    non-smoking?

You are never too old to begin anew

God gives us today to prepare for tomorrow

We really begin to live only when we are born twice

God formed us; sin deformed us; Christ transforms us

Come to Jesus for a successful heart transplant

God mends broken hearts, but he must have all the pieces

We cannot enter heaven before heaven enters us

To put your sins behind you, face them

Time is passing, and you are passing out of time

Faith is believing in advance what only makes sense
        in retrospect

God's time-out for unrepentant sinners never ends

God's bottom line: "Believe in my Son Jesus!"

You can't email your way into heaven

Many are content to live in the coal mine and never
        see the Son

Faith is the only road between my soul and heaven

God sends away empty those full of themselves

Part-time faith, like part-time jobs, cannot fully
    support you

Who I am is important, but whose I am is primary

Give your life to Christ; he can do more with it than
    you can

Jesus invested his life in you; have you shown any interest?

Those who have nothing but Christ soon learn Christ
    is enough

Have people failed you? Jesus never fails

If you don't like the way the cookie crumbles, try the
    Bread of Life

If you're going the wrong way, God allows U-turns

Believe now! Too late may come too soon!

Confession to God always brings cleansing from God

To get to heaven: It's whom you know that counts

You cannot change the truth, but the truth can change you

CAPTIONS ENCOURAGING EVANGELISM

Be winsome to win some for Christ

Gospel begins with GO

Be a channel of God's truth, not a reservoir

Evangelism is one beggar telling another where to
find bread

Millions there have never heard; millions here have
never cared

The tact needed for evangelism is contact

God had only one Son, and he was a missionary

The world has many religions, but only one Gospel

God has subpoenaed all of us as witnesses

You can never speak to the wrong person about Christ

Captions of God in Charge

Where God guides, God provides

Christ can turn your setbacks into comebacks

God often uses a setback to move us ahead

The Light of the World knows no power failure

Hope is faith holding our hand in the dark

The task ahead of us is never as great as the Power
    behind us

You can't break God's promises by leaning on them

Trust God's authority—not man's majority

All that happens to you can bring you to God

We are always in the presence of God

Faith refuses to panic because God is near

God humbles us into greatness

God's plans for us are better than our own

God has not gone on vacation and left you in charge

For a good night's rest, rest in the Lord

God supplies all our needs, one day at a time

Disappointment; his appointment

You may need to lose everything to find God is all
    you need

People fail; God rescues

To change your outlook, remember who's looking out
    for you

When you fear God, you have nothing else to fear

If Christ is your friend, you need not fear

Satan's ploys are no match for Christ's power

God is not limited by our circumstances

Peace rules the day when Christ rules the soul

If we depend on Christ for everything, we can endure anything

Tense about the future? God is always present

Where God's finger points, his hand makes the way

Fear not tomorrow; God is already there

God never closes a door without opening a window

If you make a commitment, God opens the way

When trouble blows, seek shelter in God

Our hearts are restless until they rest in God

To break sin's grip, put yourself in God's hands

God's promises have no expiration dates

When you feel hopeless, look to the God of hope

Creation bears God's autograph

Creation is a finger pointing to God

The one who upholds the world will never let you down

Write your plans in pencil but give God the eraser

The safest place to be is within the will of God

Submission to God's will is the softest pillow on which
to rest

Our needs may be great, but God is greater

Set boundaries for your life, but not for God's power

God's power comes to us when we admit our
powerlessness

God is at work even when we cannot see it

God's grace is a rainbow against even the darkest sky

When God conceals his purposes, keep living on his
promises

Faith means trusting God even if questions go
unanswered

When you have God's love, there is no room for fear

Changes can reveal God's changeless care

Even if I fail, God's love is unfailing

God can build a beautiful world out of chaos

The fear of God cancels the fear of death

Education without God is like a ship without a compass

I don't know what the future holds, but I know who holds
the future

We are always punched in on God's timecard

Test God's resources: Try the impossible

Let go and let God

God's work done God's way will never lack God's supplies

Do not measure God's mind by your own

God's lease on life never expires

God comforts us, not to make us comfortable, but to make us comforters

Bow before God, and his rainbow will surround you

Don't rely on feelings but on the Father's faithfulness

The silences of God are as eloquent as his words

You are in the driver's seat, but God holds the map

Nothing is accidental with God

God's warnings are to protect, not punish us

Captions on the Bible

Read the Bible; prevent truth decay

The Bible is not a dry book if you know the author

The future is as bright as the promises of God

The Bible: Believe it, behave it

The Bible: Read it through, work it out, pass it on

Take in the Word to keep out the world

Dusty Bibles lead to dirty lives

Apply yourself to the Bible and the Bible to yourself

BIBLE: Basic Instructions Before Leaving Earth

The mirror of God's Word is painfully clear

Feed on the Bread of Life, then serve it to others

No meal is complete without the Bread of Life

Is your Bible red or read?

The main objection against the Bible is a bad life

It is easier to debate the Bible than to obey it

The Christian's life is the world's Bible

Your life may be the only Bible some folks read

Hungry? Try feasting on God's Word

"Need directions?" God

The Bible is your best TV guide

Stand on God's Word and you won't fall into error

A well-read Bible means a well-fed soul

For a real eye-opener, open your Bible

In a changing world, trust God's unchanging Word

God's Word brings peace in the presence of pain

Addicted? Try drinking from God's Word and Spirit

Read the Bible for information and for transformation

The Bible is criticized most by those who read it least

The Bible contains the vitamins for a healthy soul

God is as good as his Word

The Bible is a compass, pointing you in the right direction

You feed your body; why starve your soul?

A Bible falling apart belongs to a person who isn't

Many books can inform; only the Bible can transform

Captions on Living a Christian Life

When growth stops, decay begins

Be rich in God, not in goods

Forgiveness gives up the right to hurt back

Be as patient with others as God is with you

Care for others because God cares for you

A world in despair needs people who care

Compassion is love in action

Our responsibility is response to his ability

Do what lets you sense God's pleasure

To master temptation, let Christ master you

We teach the Word of God by living it

A living Christ in you is a living sermon

You preach a better sermon with your life than your lips

We can preach only the Christ whom we live

Marks of a Christian: Giving and forgiving

If you stand for nothing, you will fall for anything

Do what you can today, you may not be here tomorrow

An upright man is never a downright failure

Faith: the soul's intake; love: the soul's outlet

The world crowns success; God crowns faithfulness

To know God is to love him

Concentrate on your destination, not your speed

"My way is the highway." God

Focus on a good life, not on a good living

Don't be so busy making a living that you neglect to
    make a life

A crossless life is a crownless life

Put the church in the world, not the world in the church

A living faith is a working faith

We can stop forgiving others when Christ stops
forgiving us

Those who walk with God won't run from people's needs

A changed life results from a changed heart

We "get a life" one choice at a time

To gain self-control, give Christ control

Love in deed is love indeed

Love never asks, "How much will this cost me?"

Love always seeks to help, never to hurt

To hear God's voice, turn down the world's volume

If you walk with God, you will be out of step with the world

What we sow in time we reap in eternity

What we sew in time we wear in eternity

Don't run with the world, walk with God

Overlook the faults of others, overcome your own

What on earth are you doing for heaven's sake?

Even a small light can dispel darkness

God has no hands but our hands

People who walk with God always get to their destination

Walk with God and you'll always have good company

We thank God for helping us by helping others

You don't have to be stingy with forgiveness

It takes only one candle to dispel darkness

The sweetest aroma is useless if it remains bottled up

Acts of kindness are gifts we give God

God magnifies our gifts as we use them

Give what you cannot keep and gain what you cannot lose

Reliving anger hurts only your own soul

Don't relive your anger, relieve it through forgiveness

Anger hardens the heart; forgiveness melts it

Use words to heal, not to hurt

Forgiveness is a balm for wounded hearts

A clear conscience is a soft pillow

Build bridges, not walls

Promises prayerfully made can be prayerfully kept

Keep your tongue less active and your ears more open

Keep your aim less at goods and more at goodness

Be bold in what you live for and careful of what you fall for

Is your Christianity [or faith] ancient history or current
   events?

Faith never stands around with its hands in its pockets

We should live as people prepared to die

We should die as people prepared to live

Too many saying "Our Father" live as orphans

Let your outside show a good inside

Commit the Golden Rule to memory, then commit it to life

The Golden Rule has no inches or feet, yet is the measure
    of us all

The Golden Rule works only when you make the
    first move

If Christians praise God more, the world will doubt
    him less

Lord, reform the world, beginning with me

Service for Christians is never spelled "serve-us"

True worship is not lip service but life service

When you meet temptation, turn to the right

For the road to heaven, turn right and go straight

Don't use God; ask God to use you

If on trial for your faith, would there be enough evidence
to convict you?

The heart is happiest when it beats for others

Changed lives are Christ's greatest advertisement

Love is a paint that covers others' faults

Step in to help when the world steps out

Lord, help me to be Christ to my neighbor

Doing what's right today means no regrets tomorrow

By many hands the work of God is done

God, make me worthy of my friends

Is what you're living for worth dying for?

Love is an action verb

No violinist out of sync with the conductor makes beautiful
music

Too many Christians walk by feelings, not by faith

Do great things for God, expect great things from God

It's hard to resist temptation when you go out of your way
to look for it

What really matters is what happens in us, not to us

If you serve two masters, you will always be halfhearted

The heart is an organ; keep it in tune with Jesus

Look at Jesus: the first step to leadership is servanthood

Those who put God first will be happy at last

Does your life shed light or cast shadows?

Faith is not a pill to swallow but a muscle to use

Follow the leader who follows Christ

If you have Jesus in your heart, notify your face

Live each day as if it were your last on earth

Live today as though you will face God tomorrow

Salvation makes useful saints out of useless sinners

Unclassified Christian Captions

SPORTS THEME

For a healthy heart, give your faith a workout

Is the church you attend the sports stadium?

Believing in the Yankees [*put in your own local favorite team*] won't get you eternal life

You can't lose if you stay in God's game plan

Exercise for bodily strength; worship for spiritual strength

Before you can score, you must first have a goal

Life is more fun if you don't keep score

To win in a relationship, don't keep score

God calls us to get into the game, not to keep score

You cannot win by trying to even the score

Get a home run for God by believing in Jesus

At the end of your inning, don't strike out

Life is like tennis: Serve well and you seldom lose

The one who never makes an error does not play
    much ball

One thought driven home is better than three left on base

Running from God is the longest race of all

Jesus is more precious than silver or golf

"Let's meet at my house Sunday before the game." God

The best exercise is stooping down and lifting up another

MONEY THEME

Never let gold become your God!

Give God what is right, not what is left

Deeper giving means deeper living

When it comes to giving, some people stop at nothing

The converted heart leads to an inverted purse

Without trust in God, great riches leave us in poverty

Greedy people always lose more than they gain

Live more simply that others may simply live

Better to be short of cash than short of character

Money is a good servant but a poor master

To stay out of debt, act your wage

Too often we itch for things we are not willing to
    scratch for

If outgo exceeds income, then upkeep is your downfall

Real generosity is doing something for someone who will
    never find out

Dollars do best when accompanied by some sense

If you do not enjoy what you have, you will not be happier
    with more

Money can bring you days of joy but not inner peace

Those who have God and money have no more than those who have God

We make a living by what we get; we make a life by what we give

ON SIN

The greatest sin is not to take it seriously

Christians are not sinless, but they should sin less

A small sin never stays small

Beware! Little sins grow up fast

Little sins add up to big trouble

There is no right way to do a wrong thing

Only a fool fools with sin

Unconfessed sin will fester

Those who don't believe in sin are already its victim

If you don't want the fruit of sin in your life, stay out of
   sin's orchard

The Ten Commandments are not multiple choice

UNCLASSIFIED

If you are looking for a sign from God, this is it!

When God toots, we're going to scoot

GOOD without GOD becomes O

To know Christ is to know the truth

An atheist has no invisible means of support

God promises no loaves for loafers

God can't fill someone who is full of self

One with God is a majority

Christians, like pianos, need frequent tuning

Faith expects from God what is beyond expectation

Be faithful; God will look after your success

The peace of God passes all understanding and
    misunderstanding

Those who see the invisible can do the impossible

What we weave in this world we will wear in heaven

Life makes some people better and others bitter

JOY: *J*esus first, *O*thers second, *Y*ourself last

Christianity is a pilgrim journey, not a sightseeing tour

If we wait for perfection before enjoying life, we will
    never enjoy life

Heaven is a prepared place for a prepared people

A closed mind is a door closed to God's surprises

A solitary Christian is like a fish out of water

God is the greatest teacher of forgiveness

The devil brings devastation; God offers restoration

Courage is fear conquered by love

In the Lord's work, the pay is low, but the retirement
benefits are out of this world

God measures generosity by the heart of the giver, not the
worth of the gift

Spiritual sight is as important as eyesight

God destroys the shadow of death with his Light of Life

Satan's greatest wile is "Wait a while"

God judges us by direction, not by distance

Let every ending be a new beginning

The Gospel is a declaration, not a debate

For sinners, saving grace; for Christians, serving grace

Those saved by grace should live graciously

Popularity comes from pleasing people, greatness from
pleasing God

YOUR CHURCH SIGN

To enjoy the peace of God, know the God of peace

In order to be a servant of others, master yourself

Unbelief is giving God the lie

The best things in life aren't things

God is more interested in our availability than our ability

If you don't like your lot in life, build a service station on it

Present to God your past, present, and future

Turning an inverted world upside down makes it right
side up

Goodness [*or some other quality*] is an investment that
never fails

To be alone in silence is to be alone with God

Reserve room for Jesus on your vacation [*or* business trip]

A proud person is seldom a grateful person

Even the best music has its moments of pause and rest

Faith honors God, and God honors faith

The soul that is always lighthearted misses the deepest
    things of life

Only those who give thanks for little things receive
    great things

Life is not judged by duration but by donation

Love cures people—those who both give it and receive it

Forgive and forget; sour grapes make lousy wine

God's will is not something to discover but to do

To face the future, forgive your mistakes of the past

Faith smells the fragrance when as yet there is no rose

The true end of life is to know life that never ends

There is no greater invitation to love than loving first

The task ahead is never greater than the power
    behind you

Those who give God second place give him no place

God, help me to be the person my dog thinks I am

It wasn't the apple on the tree, it was the pair beneath

The true measure of loving God is to love him without measure

We can get information online, but wisdom comes from on high

A shortcut is often a temptation in disguise

General Captions Relating to Proper Human Activity

What we love we will grow to resemble

Nothing is as strong as gentleness

When looking for faults, use a mirror, not a telescope

Instead of a critical finger, try a helping hand

Instead of pointing a finger, hold out a hand

The closest helping hand is the one at the end of your arm

You can't express love with a fist

An open hand has more power than a clenched fist

Never return a kindness; pass it on

Opportunity is often disguised as work

Behavior is the mirror in which we show our image

The oil of courtesy will save a lot of friction

If you want to break a bad habit, drop it

Master your habits, or they will master you

Cultivate good habits; the bad ones all grow wild

People do odd things to get even

Avoiding a decision is a decision

We lead best when we lead by example

No one ever climbed a rock by looking at it

Good example has twice the value of good advice

It is better to fail in doing right than to succeed in
    doing wrong

When someone does you wrong, do the right thing:
    Show love

To lighten your burdens, help others carry theirs

Judge a tree by its fruits, not by its leaves

If you are not kind, you are the wrong kind

Ordinary becomes extraordinary with just a little extra

Small deeds done are better than great deeds planned

All that's necessary for evil to win is good people doing
nothing

If you are waiting for something to turn up, start with your
shirt sleeves

The collapse of character begins on compromise corner

We stand tallest when we stoop to help another

More responsibility on your shoulders makes less room
for chips

There is no heavier load than a chip on the shoulder

A right to do something does not mean it is right

The time is always right to do what is right

Practice makes perfect, so be careful what you practice

Before trying to keep up with your neighbor, find out
where he is going

You can't get ahead when you're busy getting even

The only place success comes before work is in the
dictionary

One cannot enjoy the luxury of success without the price
of sacrifice

A leader knows the way and shows the way

When you're through improving, you're through

Victories never come at bargain prices

Commitment in the face of conflict produces character

Don't take chances; accept opportunities

It is better to wear out than to rust out

Triumph is "umph" added to try

Everyone wants to harvest but few want to plow

Ideas will not work unless you do

General Captions Relating to Proper Human Attitudes

Live with the goal in view

A good pill to swallow is pride

Swallow your pride; it's not fattening

Use self-control as your remote control

The greatest ability is dependability

People don't fail; they give up trying

Contentment consists not in great wealth but in few wants

Happiness increases the more you spread it around

Patience is a virtue that carries a lot of wait

If you brood over your troubles, you hatch despair

If you keep looking back, you can't look ahead

There are no degrees of honesty

Nothing is easy to the unwilling

You don't raise your own character by lowering others

You don't build yourself up by tearing others down

Blowing out someone else's candle doesn't make yours
    shine brighter

The person who knows everything has a lot to learn

You can't expect to see eye to eye if you look down
    on people

Nursing a grudge will never make it better

Hate: A prolonged form of suicide

A cheerful heart makes its own blue sky

Forget yourself for others, and others will never forget you

To increase your happiness, forget your neighbor's faults

The world looks brighter from behind a smile

Smile: It's gravity that holds things down

A smile adds to your face value

A smile is a curve that sets a lot of things straight

Everyone smiles in the same language

Take time to laugh; it's the music of the soul

Laughter is the shortest distance between two people

Cheerfulness oils the machinery of life

Happiness can be thought, taught, and caught,
    but not bought

Don't let yesterday use up too much of today

We are overdressed when wrapped up in ourselves

A chip on the shoulder indicates wood higher up

We who can laugh at ourselves will never cease
    to be amused

Pessimists need a kick in the can'ts

People in love with themselves have no rivals

An egotist: Someone me-deep in conversation

Those who go on ego trips travel alone

Egotism is an alphabet of one letter

Think only of yourself and others will soon forget you

The trouble with self-made persons is they worship
their creator

Learn to enjoy little things; there are so many of them

Be careful of your thoughts; they may become words at
any moment

Envy is counting someone else's blessings rather than
your own

When you're green with envy, you're ripe for trouble

Happiness comes not from your position, but your
disposition

Happiness is an inside job

Optimists make the best of it when they get the worst of it

A mind in the gutter is a life down the drain

Vows made in the storms are often forgotten in the calms

Have a heart that never hardens

Anger is only one letter away from danger

If you suppress a moment of anger, you can prevent a day
of sorrow

Many people are down on what they are not up on

Ditch dirty thoughts fast or they'll ditch you

Worry often gives small things a big shadow

Worry does not empty tomorrow of sorrow but today
of strength

Worry pulls tomorrow's cloud over today's sunshine

Fear is a dark room where negatives are developed

Procrastinators suffer from hardening of the oughteries

Much of what we see depends on what we are looking for

One who lacks courage to start has already finished

Courage is not absence of fear, but mastery over it

The worst prison is a closed heart

Always keep a cool head and a warm heart

Don't look at the world through woe-colored glasses

People who fight fire with fire end up with ashes

If you think meek is weak, try being meek for a week

The only people you should get even with are those who
    have helped you

General Captions Relating to Proper Human Speech

Gossip: The more interesting, the less likely true

Gossip travels fastest over the sour grapevine

Most gossips get caught in their own mouthtraps

Gossip is the art of saying nothing in a way that leaves nothing unsaid

Gossip is like a balloon: It grows bigger with every puff

Gossip runs down more people than cars

Carrying a tale makes a monkey out of you

Those who cook up stories will get into hot water

If it "goes without saying," don't repeat it

Words can't break bones, but they can break hearts

Speak kind words and you will hear kind echoes

Kind words are always music to a heavy heart

Be quick to praise, slow to criticize

If you growl during the day, you will be dog-tired at night

If you plant thorns, don't be surprised if you get pricked

Most entanglements are caused by vocal cords

Be a dog: Wag your tail, not your tongue

Don't leave your tongue in gear when your brain is idling

You never have to explain something you haven't said

A good way to save face is to keep the lower half closed

A closed mouth gathers no foot

It takes super strength to hold your tongue

People who fly into a rage always make bad landings

A loose tongue can get you into a tight place

Help stamp out pollution; clean up your speech!

The ability to lie is a liability

Be careful of half truths; you may be telling the wrong half

Don't stretch the truth; it may snap back at you

Nothing is opened by mistake as often as the mouth

You cannot learn and talk at the same time

Wisdom: Knowing when to speak your mind and when
    to mind your speech

One good thing you can give away and still keep:
    Your word

When we argue with fools, they're doing the same

Where one will not, two cannot quarrel

Mud thrown is ground lost

To make a mountain out of a molehill, just add dirt

Rather than find fault, find a remedy

Carve praise in stone, write criticism in sand

If you must hammer, be sure to build something

If something is laudable, make sure it's audible

If someone else blows your horn, sound travels twice
    as far

Too much complaining leaves little time for doing

Beef too much and you'll end up in a stew

A temper displayed in public is indecent exposure

Like steel, lose your temper and you lose your worth

Nothing will cook your goose faster than a red-hot temper

Have a temper that never fires

Snap judgments have a way of becoming unfastened

It is better to bite your tongue than let it bite someone else

Swallowing angry words is always easier than eating them

Keep your words sweet; you may have to eat them

Talk is cheap since the supply is greater than the demand

Don't brag: It's not the whistle that pulls the train

Words, like toothpaste, are easy to push out but hard
    to put back

Before giving someone a piece of your mind, be sure you
    can spare it

Watch your tongue: It's wet and slips easily

Other General Captions

ON FRIENDSHIP

The best antique is an old friend

Prosperity begets friends, adversity proves them

Hot words make cool friendships

We don't find friends, we make them

You can bank on friendship when interest is paid

The best vitamin for developing friends is B1

A friend is someone you can count on to count on you

A friend is someone who walks in when everyone else
walks out

A friendship is a treasure beyond measure

The ornaments of a house are the friends that frequent it

The happiest miser on earth is one who saves friends

It's smart to pick your friends—but not to pieces

UNCLASSIFIED

Follow your knows

Be present where you are

Prepare and prevent rather than repair and repent

A backbone is better than a wishbone

Trouble often starts out as fun

Problems are opportunities in disguise

Problems are opportunities in work clothes

Failure is the path of least persistence

Failure is an opportunity to begin again more intelligently

Past failures are guideposts for future successes

A sure key to failure is trying to please everybody

Success has made failures of many people

Mighty shoves move less than little pushes

A big fall begins with a little stumble

We are stronger when we stand together

Carve your name on hearts, not on marble

Seconds count, especially when dieting

For every benefit received there is a responsibility

Character is what you are in the dark

A quitter never wins, and a winner never quits

The branch that bears most fruit hangs lowest

Lost time is never found

Today is the first day of the rest of your life

Aspire to inspire before you expire

Forbidden fruit creates many jams

Every stone has its own beauty

Bloom where you are planted now

Ignorance is more costly than education

If you count your assets, you will always show a profit

Those who deserve love least need it most

People we like the least need our love the most

Patience on the road prevents patients in the hospital

You don't need references to borrow trouble

Truth does not hurt unless it ought to

Faults grow thick where love grows thin

Every day is payday in labors of love

Better to die with a good name than to live with a bad one

If you lose your temper, you can be sure no one else
    wants it

People who lose their heads are the last to miss them

Beware: Two wrongs might make a riot

Forbidden fruit may taste sweeter, but it spoils faster

You are special; become what you are

Square your walk with your talk

People may forget our speeches but follow our footsteps

Growing old is mandatory; growing up is optional

Nothing can irritate you without your permission

You cannot win respect by demanding it

Morality, like art, consists in drawing a line somewhere

It's easy to make a buck; it's tougher to make a difference

Time spent improving yourself lessens time for criticizing others

Time is the most valuable thing a person can spend

Time is precious, spend it wisely

You won't profit from your mistakes if you blame others

Those who don't make mistakes lose the chance to learn

The past should be a guide post, not a hitching post

Your past cannot be altered, but your future can

Use the past as a springboard, not a sofa

The best preparation for tomorrow is the proper use
of today

An apology is a good way to have the last word

The largest room in the world is the room for self-
improvement

If you get something for a song, watch out for the
accompaniment

It's much easier to get into trouble than out of it

If you keep courting trouble, you will soon be married to it

Not everything faced changes, but nothing changes
   unless faced

Whatever your lot, begin to cultivate it

In order to catch up, you may have to slow down

A perfectionist takes great pains and gives them to others

If you jump to conclusions, you make terrible landings

Don't put others in their place; put yourself in their place

The key is not holding good cards, but playing the ones
   you have

There are no shortcuts to any place worth going

Age is a matter of the mind: If you don't mind, it doesn't
   matter

Every journey begins with a single step

Don't crush your laurels by resting on them

Learn to say no to the good so you can say yes to the best

Too many people have sight but no vision

Vision is the art of seeing things invisible

Credibility, like credit, once lost, is hard to restore

Adversity introduces you to yourself

Although you may have pain, you don't have to be one

When you bury the hatchet, don't mark the grave

A small leak will sink a great ship

"Average" is as close to the bottom as to the top

Additional Captions

Here are several pages for you to add new captions that you have thought up or have seen in various media or while driving around in your car.

_____

_____

_____

_____

_____

_____

_____

_____

_____

_____

_____

_____

_____

_____

_____

_____

_____

_____

_____

_____

_____

_____

_____

_____

_____

_____

_____

_____

_____

_____

_____

_____

_____

We want to hear from you. Please send your comments about this book to us in care of zreview@zondervan.com. Thank you.

ZONDERVAN™

GRAND RAPIDS, MICHIGAN 49530 USA

WWW.ZONDERVAN.COM